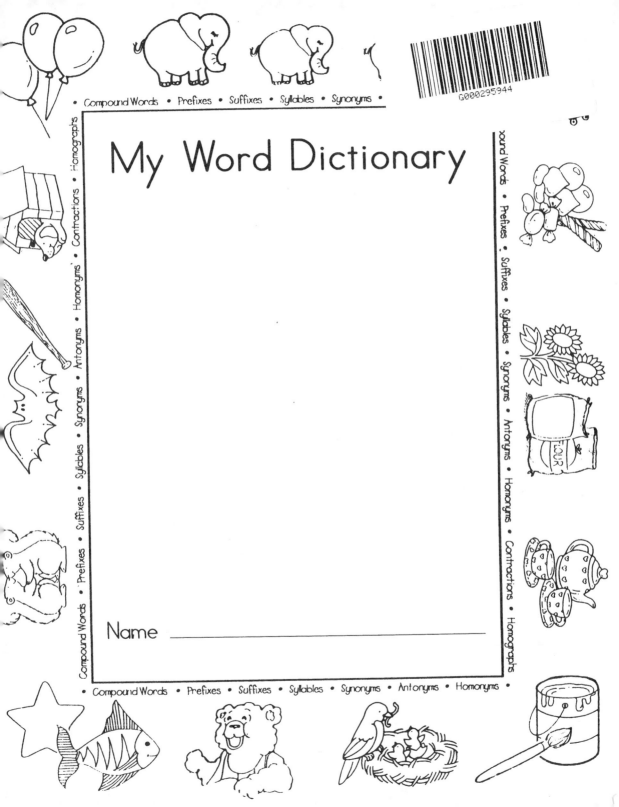

My Word Dictionary

Compound Words • Prefixes • Suffixes • Syllables • Synonyms •

Name _____

Table of Contents

Word Practice

Your *Word Dictionary* has extra lines where you can write and practice the new words you are learning. Here are some ideas:

- Choose a word to write in a sentence that has only three, four, or five words.
- Choose four words to rewrite in alphabetical order.
- Write a sentence that has three or more words from your dictionary.
- Rewrite three words. Use lines to divide them into syllables.
- Rewrite three words. Draw a circle around the base word in each.
- Choose one or more words to write in a sentence in which most of the words start with the same letter of the alphabet.
- Look through a "big" dictionary to find words to add.
- Look through newspapers and magazines to find words to add.

Compound Words

A compound word is made when two or more words are joined together to form one word.

cupcake	mailman	bathtub	starfish
baseball	mailbox	backpack	spaceship
basketball	playmate	seashell	cowboy
sunshine	snowflake	hillside	toothbrush
without	beehive	butterfly	goldfish
someone	paintbrush	popcorn	bookcase
peanut	sailboat	bedtime	rainbow
nobody	anybody	breakfast	doghouse
raincoat	anyone	pancake	teapot
weekend	daytime	milkman	rowboat
fireplace	daylight	railroad	fireplace

My Word Dictionary © Edupress EP 141

More Compound Words

_____   _____   _____

_____   _____   _____

_____   _____   _____

_____   _____   _____

_____   _____   _____

Compound Word Practice

Syllables

Words are made of syllables. You hear one vowel sound in each syllable. The vowel sound may be long, short, or blended.

One-Syllable Words		Two-Syllable Words	Three-Syllable Words
nest	fresh	habit	crocodile
once	heard	finish	gorilla
cash	throne	magic	magician
clock	strand	sweater	satellite
twist	stomp	mittens	relative
pie	teach	children	character
fruit	thought	sandwich	molecule
float	cloud	neighbor	neighborhood
key	mule	open	operate
blew	tried	soccer	magnify

_____

_____

_____

_____

_____

_____

_____

_____

_____

_____

_____

_____

My Word Dictionary © Edupress EP 141

One-Syllable Words

_____

_____

_____

_____

_____

_____

Two-Syllable Words

_____

_____

_____

_____

_____

_____

Three-Syllable Words

_____

_____

_____

_____

_____

_____

Syllable Practice

_____

_____

_____

_____

_____

_____

_____

_____

_____

_____

_____

_____

_____

Contractions

A contraction is a short way of writing two words. It is formed by leaving out one or more letters. An apostrophe (') replaces the letters that are left out.

Do not

do not	don't	he is	he's
has not	hasn't	that is	that's
is not	isn't	it is	it's
can not	can't	we are	we're
does not	doesn't	I will	I'll
did not	didn't	we will	we'll
could not	couldn't	you will	you'll
are not	aren't	you are	you're
were not	weren't	you have	you've
will not	won't	I have	I've
have not	haven't	I am	I'm

My Word Dictionary © Edupress EP 141

More Contractions

_____   _____   _____

_____   _____   _____

_____   _____   _____

_____   _____   _____

_____   _____   _____

Contraction Practice

Plural Words

Plural means "more than one." Add **s** or **ies** to a word to form the plural. There are special rules to follow.

Rule: Add **ies** to words that end in y following a consonant. First change the y to an i.

s		ies	
pencil	pencils	cherry	cherries
cap	caps	party	parties
star	stars	baby	babies
dog	dogs	lily	lilies
paper	papers	berry	berries
book	books	grocery	groceries
apple	apples	bunny	bunnies
bicycle	bicycles	lady	ladies
truck	trucks	puppy	puppies

My Word Dictionary © Edupress EP 141

More Plurals — s, ies

_____   _____   _____

_____   _____   _____

_____   _____   _____

_____   _____   _____

_____   _____   _____

Plural Practice

_____

_____

_____

_____

_____

_____

_____

_____

_____

_____

_____

Plural Words

Plural means "more than one." When **es** is added to a word it forms the plural. There are special rules to follow.

Rule: Add **es** to form the plural of words that end in **ss, x, ch,** or **sh**.

Rule: Add **es** to form the plural of words that end in **f,** or **fe**. But first change the **f** or **fe** to **v**.

glass	glasses	leaf	leaves
class	classes	calf	calves
watch	watches	knife	knives
church	churches	loaf	loaves
peach	peaches	wife	wives
dish	dishes	scarf	scarves
brush	brushes	wolf	wolves
box	boxes	shelf	shelves
ax	axes	elf	elves

_____ _____ _____

_____ _____ _____

_____ _____ _____

My Word Dictionary © Edupress EP 141

More Plurals — es

_____   _____   _____

_____   _____   _____

_____   _____   _____

_____   _____   _____

_____   _____   _____

_____   _____   _____

Plural Practice

_____

_____

_____

_____

_____

_____

_____

_____

_____

_____

_____

_____

_____

_____

Suffixes — ing ed

The suffixes **ing** and **ed** are added to a base word to describe action. There are some rules to follow.

Rule: When a short vowel word ends in a single consonant, double the consonant before adding a suffix that begins with a vowel.

ok	looking	looked
lay	playing	played
tart	starting	started
elp	helping	helped
ump	jumping	jumped
ork	working	worked
ait	waiting	waited
ugh	laughing	laughed
rush	brushing	brushed
heer	cheering	cheered

tag	tagging	tagged
rip	ripping	ripped
shop	shopping	shopped
drop	dropping	dropped
hop	hopping	hopped
plan	planning	planned
beg	begging	begged
pin	pinning	pinned

My Word Dictionary © Edupress EP 141

More Suffixes — ing, ed

_____   _____   _____

_____   _____   _____

_____   _____   _____

_____   _____   _____

_____   _____   _____

_____   _____   _____

Suffix Practice

14

Suffixes — er est

The suffixes **er** and **est** are added to a base word to make comparisons:

er compares two things

est compares more than two things

all	taller	tallest
fast	faster	fastest
soft	softer	softest
dark	darker	darkest
short	shorter	shortest
young	younger	youngest
far	farther	farthest
long	longer	longest
cold	colder	coldest
wild	wilder	wildest

er is sometimes added to a base word to mean "a person who."

sing	singer
report	reporter
teach	teacher
work	worker
farm	farmer
speak	speaker
play	player
jog	jogger

_____   _____   _____

_____   _____   _____

_____   _____   _____

My Word Dictionary © Edupress EP 141

More Suffixes — er, est

_____ _____ _____

_____ _____ _____

_____ _____ _____

_____ _____ _____

_____ _____ _____

Suffix Practice

Suffixes — ful ly less ness

A suffix is a word part that is added at the end of a base word to change its meaning or the way it is used.

ful		ly		less	
hope	hopeful	slow	slowly	care	careless
use	useful	soft	softly	harm	harmless
play	playful	loud	loudly	fear	fearless
care	careful	love	lovely	use	useless
harm	harmful	quick	quickly	sleep	sleepless

ful or less + ly			ness	
care	carefully	carelessly	loud	loudness
hope	hopefully	hopelessly	dark	darkness
fear	fearfully	fearlessly	good	goodness
harm	harmfully	harmlessly	kind	kindness

_____

_____

_____

_____

My Word Dictionary © Edupress EP 141

More Suffixes — ful, ly, less, ness

_____   _____   _____

_____   _____   _____

_____   _____   _____

_____   _____   _____

_____   _____   _____

Suffix Practice

Suffixes — y en able

A suffix is a word part that is added at the end of a base word to change its meaning or the way it is used.

y		en		able	
mp	lumpy	dark	darken	wear	wearable
ck	rocky	light	lighten	suit	suitable
irst	thirsty	fright	frighten	use	usable
ank	cranky	hard	harden	love	lovable
eep	sleepy	bright	brighten	sink	sinkable
ust	dusty			touch	touchable
rl	curly			wash	washable
ust	rusty			return	returnable
ealth	healthy				
ick	tricky				

_____   _____   _____

_____   _____   _____

_____   _____   _____

_____   _____   _____

My Word Dictionary © Edupress EP 141

More Suffixes — y, en, able

_____ _____ _____

_____ _____ _____

_____ _____ _____

_____ _____ _____

_____ _____ _____

_____ _____ _____

Suffix Practice

_____

_____

_____

_____

_____

_____

_____

_____

_____

Prefixes —dis   un

A prefix is a word part that is added at the beginning of a base word to change its meaning or the way it is used.

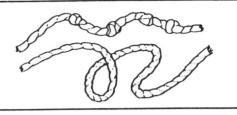

dis not		**un** not	
obey	disobey	pin	unpin
please	displease	do	undo
loyal	disloyal	dress	undress
agree	disagree	tie	untie
like	dislike	lock	unlock
trust	distrust	wrap	unwrap
able	disable	load	unload
order	disorder	happy	unhappy
appear	disappear	fair	unfair

_____   _____   _____

_____   _____   _____

_____   _____   _____

_____   _____   _____

More Prefixes — dis, un

Prefix Practice

Prefixes — re   de

A prefix is a word part that is added at the beginning of a base word to change its meaning or the way it is used.

re		de	
do again		go away from	
ͻay	repay	part	depart
ͻo	redo	tour	detour
nake	remake	plane	deplane
vrap	rewrap	train	detrain
ͻad	reload	rail	derail
vrite	rewrite	throne	dethrone
ead	reread	merit	demerit
vind	rewind	frost	defrost
ͻuild	rebuild	form	deform

_____   _____   _____

_____   _____   _____

_____   _____   _____

_____   _____   _____

My Word Dictionary © Edupress EP 141

More Prefixes — re, de, ex

_____   _____   _____

_____   _____   _____

_____   _____   _____

_____   _____   _____

_____   _____   _____

Prefix Practice

Synonyms

Synonyms are words that have the same or almost the same meaning.

big	large	laugh	giggle
happy	glad	several	many
sick	ill	look	glance
fast	quick	shout	yell
pretty	beautiful	raw	uncooked
sleepy	tired	stop	halt
sleep	rest	evening	night
noise	sound	silent	quiet
close	shut	forest	woods
nice	kind	begin	start
gift	present	angry	upset

_____   _____   _____

_____   _____   _____

_____   _____   _____

     My Word Dictionary © Edupress EP 141

More Synonyms

_____   _____   _____

_____   _____   _____

_____   _____   _____

_____   _____   _____

_____   _____   _____

_____   _____   _____

Synonym Practice

Antonyms

Antonyms are words that are opposite or almost opposite in meaning.

big	small	easy	difficult
old	new	sick	healthy
first	last	awake	asleep
strong	weak	whisper	shout
near	far	dirty	clean
thick	thin	smile	frown
deep	shallow	sharp	dull
empty	full	easy	hard
summer	winter	young	old
open	shut	walk	run
soft	hard	narrow	wide

_____   _____   _____

_____   _____   _____

_____   _____   _____

My Word Dictionary © Edupress EP 141

More Antonyms

_____   _____   _____

_____   _____   _____

_____   _____   _____

_____   _____   _____

_____   _____   _____

Antonym Practice

Homonyms

Homonyms are words that sound exactly the same but have different spellings and meanings.

	eye	tale	tail	
blue	blew	deer	dear	
see	sea	ate	eight	
here	hear	not	knot	
week	weak	write	right	
knight	night	plain	plane	
rode	road	fair	fare	
sum	some	son	sun	
sale	sail	toe	tow	
herd	heard	to	too	two
made	maid	they're	their	there

_____   _____   _____

_____   _____   _____

_____   _____   _____

My Word Dictionary © Edupress EP 141

More Homonyms

_____ _____ _____

_____ _____ _____

_____ _____ _____

_____ _____ _____

_____ _____ _____

Homonym Practice

_____

_____

_____

_____

_____

_____

_____

_____

_____

_____

_____

_____

Homographs

Homographs are words that are spelled the same way but have different meanings.

loaf	a portion of bread	spoke	have talked aloud
loaf	relax or waste time	spoke	a bar on a wheel
case	a condition or situation	prune	a dried plum
case	a container	prune	to cut off branches
bat	a flying mammal	fine	very good
bat	a wooden club	fine	money paid as a penalty
ring	a circular band	post	an upright piece of wood
ring	to make a clear sound	post	an assigned position
scale	a machine for weighing	batter	mixture of liquid and flour
scale	a series of musical tones	batter	one who hits in a game
scale	plates that cover animals	batter	to beat very hard

_____   _____   _____

_____   _____   _____

_____   _____   _____

_____   _____   _____

My Word Dictionary © Edupress EP 141

Homographs

_____   _____   _____

_____   _____   _____

_____   _____   _____

_____   _____   _____

_____   _____   _____

_____   _____   _____

Homograph Practice